Textbook for
Learning German

Glossary German – English A1

Word List:
Paul Rusch

Translation:
Angeliki Hofmann

Langenscheidt

Berlin · Munich · Vienna · Zurich · New York

© 2004 Langenscheidt KG, Berlin and Munich
Print: Druckhaus Berlin-Mitte GmbH, Berlin
Printed in Germany

ISBN-13: 978-3-468-47014-1
ISBN-10: 3-468-47014-2

6. 5. 4. 3. * 09 08 07 06

A Study Glossary – What is it?

This glossary contains all words and expressions from the textbook **Optimal A1**.
Personal names, geographical names and grammar terms are not included here.
This is a guide for effective studying techniques and suggestions.
Some of the suggested studying methods may be familiar, others are perhaps new.
They are indeed worth trying and in doing so, you will be able to decide which method is best.

Have fun learning German with **Optimal**!

The Authors

How to Use the Glossary

The glossary coincides with chapters and their parts in the textbook, accordingly.
It includes all of the necessary vocabulary for working with **Optimal A1**.
The word arrangement corresponds with the first time entry in the text book.

For help in direction, you will find the numbered chapters and their titles along with the page number in the text book.

Words appear in the following order:
1. new words from the title of the chapter
2. new words from the subtitle
3. the exercise number (A1, A2 etc.) and first words and their uses from the exercise in the margin
4. new words from the exercises from the text

The word entry includes the following information:
- noun: article and plural ending
- verb: infinitive
- accentuation: a short vowel is indicated with a dot, a long vowel is indicated with a line

A new word entry is often shown as an example either in a sentence or phrase, from the text book, written in italics, such as *Hören Sie und notieren Sie.*

Boldly printed words are from the word list of the tests from "Start Deutsch 1", level A1.

Abbreviations and Symbols

"	modified vowel forms for plural entries: *das Land, "-er*
(Pl)	noun is always or usually in the plural form: *die Leute (Pl)*
(Akk.)	accusative case
(Dat.)	dative case

Seite 6

der Mensch, -en	person
die Sprache, -n	language
das Land, "-er	country

Name, Herkunft, Sprache

der Name, -n	name
die Herkunft	origin

A1 **die Information, -en**	information
zu	about
die Person, -en	person
hören	to listen
Sie	you
und	and
notieren	to jot down, to make a note of 7
Hören Sie und notieren Sie.	Listen and jot down.
der Wohnort, -e	place of residence, address
gut	good
der Tag, -e	day
Guten Tag!	Hello!
Servus!	Hi!
Grüezi!	Hi!
noch	again, more
einmal	once
noch einmal	once again
lesen	to read
Lesen Sie.	Read.
sagen	to say
Andrea sagt „Guten Tag!"	Andrea says "Hello!"
kommen	to come
aus	from
Deutschland	Germany
Andrea kommt aus Deutschland.	Andrea comes from Germany.
wohnen	to live
in	in
Sie wohnt in Hamburg.	She lives in Hamburg.

spr**e**chen	to speak
D**eu**tsch	German
Englisch	English
Sie spricht Deutsch und	She speaks German and
Englisch.	English.
Österreich	Austria
Ital**ie**nisch	Italian
er	he
die Schw**ei**z	Switzerland
Er kommt aus der Schweiz.	He comes from Switzerland.
Franz**ö**sisch	French
Sp**a**nisch	Spanish
alle	all
dr**ei**	three
aber	but, yet, however
versch**ie**den	different
Alle drei sprechen Deutsch,	All three speak German,
aber verschieden.	yet differently.

Seite 7

A3 fr**a**gen	to ask
im (= in dem)	in, in the
Fragen Sie im Kurs	Ask in class.
m**a**chen	to make, to prepare, to arrange
das Portr**ä**t, -s	portrait, description

Tip

Pronouncing names in German

Many words are seemingly similar in different languages, in particular personal names. This is a good opportunity to compare the similarity in German to other languages. Say these words out loud.

German	Your Language	Other Languages, for example: English, Swedish.
der Tag, Tage	_____	day

Be careful: The pronounciation can vary with different accents on different syllables. Mark the accented syllable in the German word and compare this to yours or another language.

Alphab**e**t, Adr**e**sse, Telef**o**nnummer, Z**e**ntrum, N**o**rden, W**e**sten . . .
Am**e**rika, Austr**a**lien, Eur**o**pa, **E**ngland, Schw**ei**z, **Ö**sterreich, Sp**a**nien, It**a**lien, M**ü**nchen, Z**ü**rich, W**ie**n . . .

Machen Sie Porträts.	Write a description.
ạntworten	to answer
Hạllo.	Hello.
wie	how
heißen	to be called
du	you
Hallo, wie heißt du?	Hello, what is your name?
ịch	I
Ich heiße Martina.	My name is Martina.
wohẹr?	where (from)?
Woher kommst du?	Where are you from?
Woher kommen Sie?	Where are you from?
wọ?	where?
Wo wohnst du?	Where do you live?
wẹlch-?	what, which?
Welche Sprachen sprichst du?	What languages do you speak?

Seite 8

Adresse, Telefonnummer

die Adrẹsse, -n	address
die Telefọnnummer, -n	telephone number

A 4 begrüßen	to greet
vọrstellen	to introduce
dịe (Pl)	the
Wie heißen die Personen?	What are the people's names?
	Who are these people?

Tip

Memorize frequently used questions and answers.

Make a note of the usual questions and answers and jot down the accents.
Read these sentences at home, at best in front of a mirror.

Learn these questions and answers by heart.
Mark and remember the melody of the sentence.

Woher <u>kommst</u> du? ↗	Ich komme aus . . .
Wo wohnst du?	Ich wohne in . . .
Welche Sprache sprichst du?	Ich spreche . . .
Wie ist die Adresse?	. . .
Wie ist bitte die Telefonnummer?	. . .

sein	to be
Guten Tag, ich bin Gertrud Steiner.	Hello, I am Gertrud Steiner.
angenehm	Nice to meet you.
der Herr, -en	Mr.
Woher kommen Sie, Herr Papadopoulos?	Mr. Papadopoulos, where are you from?
liegen	to be located in
der Westen	west
von	of
Das liegt im Westen von Griechenland.	That is located in the western part of Greece.
Aha!	I see.
Lateinamerika	South America
A 5 die Zahl, -en	number
die Postleitzahl, -en	zip code, postcode
danke	thank you
Danke, und wie ist die Adresse?	Thank you, and what is the address?
viel	many
der Dank	thank
Vielen Dank.	Many thanks.
A 6 ein	a, an
das Interview, -s	interview
der Partner, –	partner
die Partnerin, -nen	partner
wer?	who?
das	this, that
Wer ist das? – Das ist Bruno.	Who is this? – This is Bruno.
bitte	please

Seite 9

Training

das Training	practice

Informationen suchen und ordnen

suchen	to look for, to search for
ordnen	to order, to arrange
Informationen suchen und ordnen	Search for and arrange the information.

mein — my

Mein Name ist Werner. — My name is Werner.

die Comicfigur — cartoon character

der Norden — north

der — the

der Vorname, -n — first name

deutsch — German

leben — to live

Ich lebe in Österreich, — I live in Austria,

in Innsbruck. — in Innsbruck.

die Japanerin, -nen — Japanese

die Österreicherin, -nen — Austrian

lernen — to learn

Sergei lernt Deutsch. — Sergei is learning German.

die Familie, -n — family

das Zentrum, Zentren — center

bisschen — some, a little (bit)

Er spricht ein bisschen — He speaks a little bit of

Deutsch. — German.

das Telefon, -e — telephone

Seite 10

Wortschatz

der Wortschatz — vocabulary

Kontinente, Länder, Sprachen

der Kontinent, -e — continent

A 10 spielen — to play, to act out

Spielen Sie. — Act out the situation.

Deutsch lernen

A 11 das Wort, "-er — word

schreiben — to write

Schreiben Sie. — Write.

diskutieren — to discuss

Diskutieren Sie. — Discuss.

markieren — to mark

Markieren Sie das Wort. — Mark the word.

zuordnen — to match

Ordnen Sie die Bilder zu. — Match the words with the pictures.

Seite 11

Aussprache

die <u>Au</u>ssprache   pronounciation

Akzent, Pause, Sprechmelodie

der S<u>a</u>tz, "-e   sentence

Seite 12

Grammatik

die Gramm<u>a</u>tik   grammar

A 17   vergl<u>ei</u>chen   to compare
Schreiben Sie und ver-   Write and compare.
gleichen Sie.

A 18   <u>o</u>der   or

Personen ansprechen: „du" oder „Sie"

A 18   das B<u>i</u>ld, -er   drawing, illustration,
                           picture
der Dial<u>og</u>, -e   dialogue

---

2   Eine fremde Stadt

Seite 14
fr<u>e</u>md   foreign, unfamiliar
die St<u>a</u>dt, "-e   city, town

Ankunft

die <u>A</u>nkunft   arrival

A 1   inform<u>ie</u>ren (sich)   to inform (yourself) about,
                                   to find out about (some-
                                   thing)

w<u>a</u>s?   what?
die Fr<u>au</u>, -en   woman
Entsch<u>u</u>ldigung.   Excuse me.
j<u>a</u>   yes
Ja, bitte?   Yes, please?

die Touristeninforma-tion, -en	tourist information
der Moment, -e	moment
m_al	just
Moment mal!	Just a moment.
s_ehen	to look
d_a	there
der Ausgang, "-e	exit
Sehen Sie: Da ist der Ausgang.	Look, there is the exit.
g_ehen	to go
geradeaus	straight ahead
ungefähr	about
der Meter, –	meter
Gehen Sie da geradeaus, ungefähr 100 Meter.	Go straight ahead for about 100 meters.
f_inden	to find
r_echts	right
Da finden Sie rechts die Touristeninformation.	There, on the right, you will find the tourist information.
A2 möcht-	like, wish for
der Stadtplan, "-e	map of the city
Ich möchte einen Stadtplan.	I would like to have a map of the city.
h_ier	here
Hier, bitte.	Here you are, please.
h_aben	to have
auch	also
das Kulturprogramm	pamphlet for cultural events
Haben Sie auch ein Kultur-programm?	Have you also got a pam-phlet for cultural events?
der Stadtprospekt, -e	city brochure
das Touristen-Ticket, -s	tourist ticket
n_ein	no
leider	unfortunately
n_icht	not
Nein, leider nicht.	No, unfortunately not.
das Ticket, -s	ticket
g_eben	to give, to be available
es gibt	there is/are
der Bahnhof, "-e	train station
Tickets gibt es im Bahnhof.	There are tickets available at the train station.
das Hotel, -s	hotel

A3 orientieren (sich)   to get one's bearings, to orientate oneself

Er orientiert sich auf dem Stadtplan.   He is getting his bearings by the city map.

der Weg, -e   way, route
die Straße, -n   street
die Allee, -n   avenue

A4 lange   long
brauchen   to require, to take
Wie lange braucht die Frau?   How long does the woman take?

ganz   very
einfach   easy
Das ist ganz einfach.   That is very easy.
wir   we
die Richtung, -en   direction
Gehen Sie Richtung Zentrum.   Go in the direction of the center.

links   left
das Theater, –   theater
weitergehen   to continue on
Sie gehen rechts weiter.   Continue to go right.
dann   then
der Platz, "-e   square, plaza
dort   there, that
beginnen   to start, to begin
Dort beginnt die Logenstraße.   That is where Logenstraße starts.

weit   far (from here)
Ist das weit?   Is it far from here?
nur   only
bis   to
die Minute, -n   minute
Sie gehen nur 5 bis 10 Minuten.   It's only a 5 to 10 minute walk.

Im Hotel

A5 anmelden (sich)   to register (oneself)
sich im Hotel anmelden   to register in the hotel
bleiben   to stay

Wie lange bleibt die Frau?	How long is the woman staying?
variieren	to change around
Variieren Sie den Dialog.	Change the conversation around.
man	one
Wie schreibt man das?	How does one write that?
mit	with
am (= **an** dem)	at the
der Anfang, "-e	beginning
Mit „Ha-el" am Anfang.	With "h-l" at the beginning.
ach	oh
das Einzelzimmer, –	single room
die Nacht, "-e	night
stimmen	to be correct
Stimmt das, Frau Hlasek?	Is that correct, Frau Hlasek?
richtig	yes, right
unterschreiben	to sign
Bitte hier unterschreiben.	Please sign here.
der Schlüssel, –	key
das Zimmer, –	room
das Frühstück	breakfast
von . . . bis	from . . . to
die Uhr, -en	clock
Frühstück gibt es von sieben bis zehn Uhr.	Breakfast is from seven to ten o'clock.
das Meldeformular, -e	registration form
der Gast, "-e	guest
die Firma, -en	company
das Telefax, -e	fax
die E-Mail-Adresse, -n	e-mail address
das Datum, -en	date
die Unterschrift, -en	signature
A 6 beschreiben	to explain
auf	on
Beschreiben Sie einen Weg auf dem Stadtplan.	Explain a route on the city map.
der Ort, -e	place, location
gerne	certainly, with pleasure

Seite 16

Ein Tag in Essen

austauschen | to exchange
Informationen austauschen | Exchange information
interessieren | to be of interest
Was interessiert Sie? | What are you interested in?
sammeln | to collect
Sammeln Sie Wörter. | Collect words.
das Musik-Theater, – | theater for music and dance
die Oper, -n | opera
das Ballett | ballet
erbauen | to build, to construct
der Stadtgarten, "– | city park
der Süden | south
groß | large
der Park, -s | park
die Halle, -n | hall
der Sport | sport
das Konzert, -e | concert
die Ausstellung, -en | exhibition
das Museum, -en | museum
die Grafik, -en | graphic arts
die Skulptur, -en | sculpture
das Jahrhundert, -e | century
die Fotografie, -n | photography
die Sammlung, -en | collection
Fotografie-Sammlung | photography collection
alt | old
die Synagoge, -n | synagogue, temple
der Nazi, -s | Nazi
zerstören | to destroy
von den Nazis zerstört | destroyed by the Nazis ·
jetzt | now, today
die Zeche, -n | coalpit
die Kohleindustrie | coal industry
das Kulturzentrum, | cultural center
 -zentren |
das UNESCO-Kulturerbe | cultural heritage of the UNESCO

zusammen | together
Was machen Milena und | What are Milena and
 Beatrix zusammen? | Beatrix doing together?
besuchen | to visit
die Freundin, -nen | girlfriend
Milena besucht eine | Milena is visiting a girl-
 Freundin in Essen. | friend in Essen.

der Prospekt, -e	leaflet, brochure
der Plan, "-e	plan
Sie lesen Prospekte und machen Pläne.	They are reading leaflets and making plans.
morgen	tomorrow
die Zeit	time
Hast du morgen Zeit, Beatrix?	Have you got time tomorrow, Beatrix?
viel	much
nicht viel	not much
die Stunde, -n	hour
zuerst	first, at first
die Altstadt	old town
Wir gehen zuerst in die Altstadt.	First, we will go to the old town.
das Münster, –	cathedral
sehr	very
bekannt	well-known
Die Alte Synagoge ist sehr bekannt.	The old synagogue is very well-known.
zum (= zu dem)	to the
allein	by oneself, single handed
Das findest du auch allein.	You can also find that by yourself.
die Fotoausstellung, -en	photography exhibition
toll	great, wonderful, terrific
abends	in the evening
um	at
um 7 Uhr abends	at 7 o'clock in the evening
oh	oh
schön	good, fine, splendid
Oh, das ist schön	Oh, that is fine.

A9 Ihr-	your
Stellen Sie Ihre Stadt vor.	Introduce your city to us.

Seite 17

Internationale Wörter suchen

international	international

A 10 die Musik	music
das Foto, -s	photograph

```
==========================================
| European Bookshop          Phone:  020-7734-5259
| 5 Warwick Street           Fax:    020-7287-1720
| London, W1B 5LU                    www.EuropeanBookshop.com
==========================================
|                                    Date 05/02/07 14:35  Asst AMF
|                                    R/O  R RECEIPT  Number 695232
| CUSTOMER/DELIVERY ADDRESS
|                                    VAT Number 274 4347 47
| Counter Sale
|                     Ref/Tel.                        Terms  10.00
==========================================
| EAN              Code    Author/Title       Series   Qty  Price VAT
| 9783468470141    13883   OPTIMAL A1/GLOSSAR  OPMA      1   5.35  1
==========================================
| Items    VAT RATE    1    0.00%   Goods     VAT      Total
|     1    Value            4.81             0.00      4.81
==========================================
| Type [ 2]  2=CSH 3=CHQ 4=CRCD 5=VCHR 6=ePDQ   Currency [ 5] Sterling
| Exchange rate  1.0000 Amount tendered  10.01   Change GBP        5.20
| Cheque/Credit Card Number                      Expiry    MM      YY
==========================================
```

z**u**	going with, concerning
das Th**e**ma, -en	theme, topic
der B**ea**ch-Volleyball	beach volleyball
der Sp**i**tzensport	top sport
dir**e**kt	directly
das M**u**sical, -s	musical
der W**e**lterfolg, -e	world-renowned
der Musical-Welterfolg	world-renowned musical
das Le**ben**	life
Die K**a**iserin, -nen	empress
der M**ei**sterfotograf, -en	master photographer
der Tr**e**ffpunkt, -e	meeting place
das F**i**lmfestival, -s	film festival
für	for
der F**i**lmfreund, -e	film enthusiast
der Fi**lm, -e**	film, movie
die Fei**er, -n**	celebration
das Kult**u**rfest, -e	cultural festival
das F**e**st, -e	festival
der T**a**nz, "-e	dance
die Spezialit**ä**t, -en	speciality
die Kult**u**r, -en	culture
das Jugendzentrum, -zentren	youth center
das Lie**d, -er**	song
die **E**rde	earth
n**a**ch	from, according to
Ballett nach der Musik von Gustav Mahler	Ballet from the music of Gustav Mahler

Um Wiederholung bitten

die Wiederh**o**lung, -en	repetition
b**i**tten	to ask for, to request
um Wiederholung bitten	to ask for a repetition

A 11 der M**a**nn, "-er	man
buchstab**ie**ren	to spell
Buchstabieren Sie die Namen.	Spell the names.
w**i**ssen	to know, to be familiar with
d**o**ch	for sure, certainly, surely
Du weißt doch, Beach-Volleyball.	Surely, you're familiar with beach volleyball.
die Or**a**nger**ie**	orangery, conservatory

die Orange, -n	orange
so	like that
Ach so.	Oh, I see.
langsam	slowly

A 12 wählen	to choose
das Programm, -e	program
Wählen Sie ein Programm.	Choose a program.

Seite 18

Wörter auf dem Stadtplan

A 13 das Kino, -s	movie theater, cinema
die Kirche, -n	church
die Post	post office
die Gasse, -n	lane
das Rathaus, "-er	city hall

A 14 **die Farbe, -n**	color
maskulin: **der**	masculine
neutrum: **das**	neutral
feminin: **die**	feminine

Hotelreservierung

die Hotelreservierung, -en	hotel reservation

Tip

Get to know the noun with the article – use colors.

Choose three colors, one for every article. Always use one of the three colors for both noun and article.
If words belong to a particular picture or drawing, mark this picture with the same color also.

die Post
die Straße
der Park
das Kino

A 15 ausfüllen	to complete, to fill in
das Formular, -e	form
Füllen Sie das Formular aus.	Complete this form.
die Reservierung, -en	reservation
der Preis, -e	price
das Doppelzimmer, –	double room
die Dusche, -en	shower
ohne	without
das Bad, "-er	bath
ohne Dusche/Bad	without bath
maximal	maximum
der Euro, -s	Euro
der Familienname, -n	surname, last name
die Nummer, -n	number
das Fax	fax

A 16 die Homepage, -s	homepage

Seite 19

Akzent und Sprechmelodie

die Aussage, -n	statement
nachfragen	to inquire

Schwierige Wörter aussprechen

schwierig	difficult
schwierige Wörter	to pronounce difficult
aussprechen	words

Satz: Ja-/Nein-Frage und W-Frage

die Antwort, -en   answer

Verb und Subjekt: Konjugation Präsens

sie (Pl)   they
Sie gehen in die Altstadt.   They walk to the old town.

3   Musik

Das Konzert

A1 heiß	hot
die Leute (Pl)	people
da sein	to be there
Viele Leute sind da.	Many people are there.
die Bühne, -n	stage
dunkel	dark
das Licht, -er	light
angehen	to turn on, to go on
Das Licht geht an.	The lights go on.
stehen	to be (situated on)
die Band, -s	band
Auf der Bühne steht eine Band.	On the stage there is a band.
die Mitte	middle
in der Mitte	in the middle
Rockmusik	rock music
Sie spielen Rockmusik.	They play rock music.
komponieren	to compose
Ballettmusik	ballet music
Sie komponieren Ballettmusik.	They compose ballet music.
produzieren	to produce
die CD, -s	CD, compact disk
Sie produzieren CDs.	They produce CDs.

A2 das Alter	age
das Instrument, -e	instrument
die Frage, -n	question
okay	okay
der Sänger, –	singer
singen	to sing
schon	already, so far
Wie lange singst du schon?	How long have you been singing?
das Jahr, -e	year
spielen	to play
Spielst du auch ein Instrument?	Do you also play an instrument?
natürlich	sure, of course
die Gitarre, -n	guitar

Im Studio: Zahlen und Musik

das Studio, -s	studio

A3 der Computer, –	computer
das Mikrofon, -e	microphone
das Musikinstrument, -e	musical instrument
das Experiment, -e	experiment
mischen	to mix
Er mischt Zahlen und Musik.	He mixes numbers and music.

Seite 23

Die Welt-Tour

die Welt, -en	world
die Tour, -en	tour

A4 der März	March
wohin?	where (to)?
der Juni	June
Wohin gehen sie im Juni?	Where are they going in June?
unterwegs	on the road

der Monat, -e	month
starten	to start, to begin
Europa	**Europe**
Sie starten in Europa.	They begin in Europe.

der Januar	January
der Mai	May
die Woche, -n	week
nach	towards, to
der August	August
fliegen	to fly
Sie fliegen nach Asien.	They fly to Asia.
der September	September
der Oktober	October
wieder	again
der November	November
der Dezember	December
frei	off
Sie haben frei.	They have the time off.
der April	April
der Februar	February

A 5 wann?	when
Wann sind sie in Deutsch-land?	When are they in Germany?
die Radiomeldung, -en	radio report, radio announcement
der Tour-Plan, "-e	tour schedule
anders	different
der Montag	Monday
der Sonntag	Sunday
das Wochenende, -n	weekend
der Dienstag	Tuesday
der Mittwoch	Wednesday
der Donnerstag	Thursday
der Freitag	Friday
der Samstag	Saturday

Seite 24

Das Mozart Quartett Salzburg

das Quartett, -s	quartet

A 7 seit	since
seit 1996	since 1996
der Musiker, –	musician
die Musikerin, -nen	musician
(die) Klassik	classical music

Die Musiker spielen Klassik.	The musicians play classical music.
die Violine, -n	violin
daneben	next to
bei	by, in the area of, near
bei Hamburg	near Hamburg
die Viola, Violen	viola
das Violoncello, -celli	cello
heute	these days
auftreten	to appear (in concert)
das Inland	nation, within the country
das Ausland	foreign country
Sie treten im In- und Ausland auf.	They appear in concerts, internationally and nationally.
das Stück, -e	piece
unterstützen	to support
die Schule, -n	school
Afrika	Africa
Das Quartett unterstützt Schulen in Afrika.	The quartet supports schools in Africa.
die Initiative, -n	project
spenden	to donate
pro	per
Die Musiker spenden 5 Euro pro CD.	The musicians donate 5 Euros per CD.
der Schüler, –	student
die Schülerin, -nen	student
kaufen	to buy
das Buch, "-er	book
Sie kaufen Bücher.	They buy books.
das Heft, -e	notebook
der Bleistift, -e	pencil

Tip

Learning words and their forms

Automatically learn the noun with the article, as well as its plural form, together.

die Musikerin / die Musikerinnen
das Musikinstrument / die Musikinstrumente

Write example sentences:

Die Musikerinnen suchen die Musikinstrumente.

After a few days, test your knowledge to see if you still remember the form. If you repeat regularly, you are less likely to forget.

Musik, Musik, Musik

A 8	über	about
	über Musik sprechen	to talk about music
	finden	to think of, to consider
	Wie findest du das Konzert?	What do you think of the concert?
	spitze	excellent
	gut	good
	super	terrific

schlecht	terrible, not good, bad
die Katastrophe, -n	catastrophe
Der Sänger ist eine Katastrophe.	The singer is a catastrophe.
denn	then
Welche Musik hörst du denn gerne?	What music do you like to listen to?
mögen	to prefer, to like
Jazz	jazz
lieber	rather
(der) Rock	rock music
Ich mag lieber Rock.	I rather prefer rock music.
das Violinkonzert, -e	violin concert
die Solistin, -nen	soloist

A 9	das Gefallen	preference, pleasure
	ausdrücken	to express
	Gefallen ausdrücken	Expressing preferences
	(die) Volksmusik	folk music
	(das/der) Techno	techno music

Seite 25

Texte verstehen: W-Fragen

der Text, -e	text
verstehen	to understand
Texte verstehen	understanding texts

A 10	nach	after
	die Pause, -n	rest, break (in time)
	nach der Pause	after the break
	die Platte, -n	record
	der Star, -s	star
	vor	in front of
	das Stadion, Stadien	stadium
	als	as the
	als erster deutscher Musiker	as the first German musician
	der Fan, -s	fan
	das Internet	internet

Reading efficiently with question words

Question words or W-words always help you to find out about people, time, place, activity or condition. Begin by reading the text several times. After the first time, jot down the answers to the question *Wer?* After the second reading mark the answers to *Wo?* Then follow up with *Wann?* and *Was?*
Divide the text up into parts and note the information accordingly.

> Vertreter von 180 Staaten treffen sich auf der Klima-Konferenz in Mailand vom 1.–12. Dezember.
> Klimaschutz durch weniger Treibhausgase – das ist der zentrale Gedanke. Laut Kyoto-Protokoll müssen die Industrieländer ihre Treibhausgase bis 2012 um 5,2 Prozent im Vergleich zu 1990 vermindern.

(section)	**Wer?**	**Wo?**	**Wann?**	**Was?**
(1)	180 Staaten	Mailand	1.–12.12.	Klima-Konferenz
(2)				

Seite 26

Musik

A 12	die Mind-map	mind map
	zeichnen	to draw
	Zeichnen Sie Ihre Mind-map.	Draw your own mind map.
	der Stil, -e	style
	das Cello, Celli	cello
	der Sampler, –	sampler
	das Schlagzeug, -e	drums
	der Pianist, -en	pianist
	die Pianistin, -nen	pianist
	die Sängerin, -nen	singer

Datum, Monate, Wochentage

	der Wochentag, -e	weekday
A 13	der Unterschied, -e	difference
	die Regelmäßigkeit, -en	regularity

Time – Weekdays/Dates – Months – Years

Arrange expressions of time in *im* ..., *am* ..., *um* ....
Make a note of personal dates and read them out loud,
to yourself, at home.

im + season and month
Im Herbst gehe ich nach Deutschland.
Ich habe **im** April Geburtstag.

am + weekday/date
Ich habe **am** 8. April Geburtstag.
Am Montag habe ich Deutsch.

um + time
Ich stehe **um** halb acht auf.
Der Deutschkurs beginnt **um** 16.15 Uhr.

A 15 der Geburtstag, -e	birthday
Wann haben Sie Geburtstag?	When is your birthday?
wichtig	important

Seite 27

A 16 wunderbar	wonderful
blöd	silly, stupid

---

4 Tagesablauf – Arbeit – Freizeit

Seite 30

der Tagesablauf, "-e	daily routine
die Arbeit, -en	work, employment, job
die Freizeit	leisure time, spare time

Am Morgen

der Morgen, –	morning

A 1 passieren	to happen, to take place
Was passiert?	What happens?
erzählen	to tell, to explain
Erzählen Sie.	Explain.
klingeln	to ring
der Wecker, –	alarm clock

Um 6 Uhr klingelt der Wecker.	The alarm clock rings at 6 o'clock.
<u>au</u>fstehen	to get up
Sie steht nicht gerne auf.	She does not like getting up.
l<u>ie</u>gen bleiben	to stay in bed, to remain in bed
Sie bleibt noch einen Moment liegen.	She stays in bed a moment longer.
das R<u>a</u>dio, -s	radio
das V<u>ie</u>rtel, –	quarter
Viertel nach sechs	*quarter past six*
d<u>u</u>schen	to shower
Zuerst duscht sie.	First, she showers.
h<u>o</u>len	to get, to fetch
die Z<u>ei</u>tung, -en	newspaper
Dann holt sie die Zeitung.	Then she gets the newspaper.
k<u>o</u>chen	to boil, to prepare
das W<u>a</u>sser	water
der K<u>a</u>ffee	coffee
Sie kocht Kaffee.	She makes coffee.
<u>e</u>twa	about, around
fr<u>ü</u>hstücken	to have breakfast
Etwa um sieben Uhr frühstückt sie.	At about 7 o'clock she has breakfast.
<u>e</u>ssen	to eat

Tip

Learning verbs by putting them in chronological order

Place verbs and expressions in chronological order. Ask yourself: What do I do first? What happens then? What comes next? . . . What happens at the end? Put these action words in chain order, trying not to make your chain too long.

Arrange the chains with arrows and give each chain a title.

Alltag

aufstehen → anziehen → frühstücken → Zähne putzen → weggehen → die Türe schließen → den Bus nehmen →

Learn words in phrases.

Jot these phrases down on a card. Turn the card over and write a sentence in the first person.

Zeitung lesen	Ich lese Zeitung.
Kaffee trinken	Zum Frühstück trinke ich Kaffee.
bei der Abendpost arbeiten	
ein Porträt machen	
in der Nacht arbeiten	
viel verdienen	

die Cornflakes (Pl)	cornflakes
Sie isst Cornflakes.	She eats cornflakes.
losgehen	to leave, to go, to start
Sie geht los.	She leaves.
schließen	to close, to lock
die Tür, -en	door
Sie schließt die Tür.	She closes the door.
rennen	to run
zur (= zu der)	to the underground /
die U-Bahn, -en	subway
Sie rennt zur U-Bahn.	She runs to the under-ground.
abfahren	to depart, to leave
genau	exactly
Die U-Bahn fährt genau um 7 Uhr 30 ab.	The underground leaves at 7:30 sharp.
voll	full, packed
kein-	not any, not one

Learn the separable verbs.

Learn the separable verbs by emphasizing the accent on the proper syllable. Write these verbs on small cards. Turn the card over and write a short sentence with the verb in the first person.

aufstehen	Ich stehe um 7.00 Uhr auf.
weggehen	Ich gehe um 8.30 weg.
ankommen	
einkaufen	

der Pl<u>a</u>tz, "-e	seat
<u>a</u>nkommen	to arrive
das St<u>a</u>dtzentrum, -zentren	center of the city
Die U2 kommt im Stadt-	The U2 arrives at the
zentrum an.	center of the city.
die <u>U</u>-Bahn-Station, -en	underground station,
	subway station
<u>au</u>ssteigen	to get out
Sara steigt aus.	Sara gets out.
der F<u>u</u>ß, "-e	foot
Sie geht zu Fuß weiter.	She goes on by foot. / She
	walks the rest.

Im Büro

das Bür<u>o</u>, -s	office

A 2 ver<u>a</u>bschieden (sich)	to say goodbye (to someone)
die Redakti<u>o</u>n, -en	editor's office
<u>a</u>rbeiten	to work
Hier arbeitet sie.	She works here.
der Fl<u>u</u>r, -e	corridor, hall
tr<u>e</u>ffen	to meet
die Ch<u>e</u>fin	supervisor, boss
Im Flur trifft sie die Chefin.	She meets the supervisor in
	the hall.
Guten M<u>o</u>rgen!	Good morning.
g<u>e</u>hen	to go, to happen, to turn out
<u>I</u>hnen (Dat.)	you
Wie geht es Ihnen?	How are you?
die S<u>ei</u>te, -n	page
die Fotogr<u>a</u>fin, -nen	photographer
die Journal<u>i</u>stin, -nen	journalist
der Stud<u>e</u>nt, -en	student
der N<u>a</u>chtportier, -s	evening porter
die <u>E</u>-Mail, -s	e-mail

A 3 der Term<u>i</u>n, -e	appointment
ver<u>ei</u>nbaren	to arrange
das Term<u>i</u>nproblem, -e	problem with an appoint-
	ment
das Caf<u>é</u>, -s	café, coffee shop
möglich	possible
Der Termin um 14 Uhr ist	The appointment for
nicht möglich.	2 o'clock is not possible.

k**u**rz	quick
bitte kurz antworten	give a short answer
das Proble**m, -e**	problem
kein Problem	no problem

Seite 31

Das Interview

A 4 v**o**r	before
vor dem Interview	before the interview
v**o**rbereiten	to prepare for
Sara Becker bereitet	Sara Becker prepares for
das Interview vor.	the interview.
brau**chen**	to need
die K**a**mera, -s	camera
der Fi**lm, -e**	film
Sie braucht die Kamera	She needs the camera and
und Filme.	film.
das Kass**e**ttengerät, -e	cassette recorder, tape recorder
verg**e**ssen	to forget
Das Kassettengerät nicht	Don't forget the tape
vergessen!	recorder!
die Not**i**z, -en	note, comment

A 5 der Tr**au**mberuf, -e	ideal job
das Stu**dium, St**u**dien**	education, studies
der Freu**nd, -e**	friend
das Ge**ld**	money
der Lo**hn, "-e**	wage, pay

A 6 die T**ä**tigkeit, -en	occupation
der Nachmitta**g, -e**	afternoon
zur**ü**ck	return
Sie ist zurück im Büro.	She returns to the office.
ansehen	to look at
Zuerst sieht sie die Fotos an.	First she looks at the photos.
gefa**llen**	to like, to please
ihr (Dat.)	her
Zwei Fotos gefallen ihr gut.	She is pleased with two photos.
der Art**i**kel, –	article
fe**rtig**	finished

Der Artikel ist fertig.	The article is finished.
müde	tired
zufrieden	content, satisfied
einkaufen	to shop, to go shopping
Sie kauft ein.	She goes shopping.
das Haus, "-er	house
nach Hause	home
Sie geht nach Hause.	She goes home.
der Abend, -e	evening
der Salat, -e	salad
das Sandwich, -(e)s	sandwich
fernsehen	to watch television
Sie sieht noch ein bisschen *fern.*	She watches some televi- sion.
der Krimi, -s	thriller
die Nachrichten	news
die Nachrichten sehen	to watch the news
schlafen	to sleep
Sie schläft.	She sleeps.
Sie geht schlafen.	She goes to bed.

Tip

Studying words in groups

Write down about seven words according to a topic and place these words, at random, around the topic. Learn them in relation to each other.

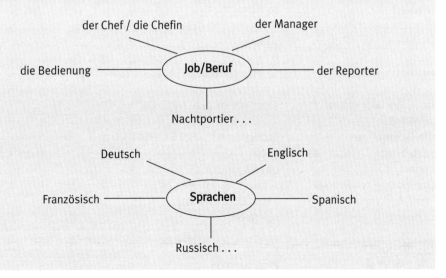

A7 das Gespräch, -e	conversation
alles	everything, all
Ist alles okay?	Is everything okay?
das Glück	luck
Viel Glück und auf Wiedersehen!	Lots of luck and good-bye.
ausmachen	to arrange
einen Termin ausmachen	to arrange an appointment
tun	to do
Leid tun	to be sorry for, to regret
Das tut mir Leid.	I'm sorry.
gehen	to accept, to allow
Geht 15.00 Uhr?	Is 3:00 p.m. okay?
bald	soon, then
Bis bald.	See you then.
Tschüs!	Bye.

Seite 32

Freizeit

A8 der Mittag, -e	noon, midday
Samstagmittag	Saturday noon
frei haben	to have off (from work)
Sie hat frei.	She has time off.
spazieren gehen	to go for a walk
Sie geht im Park spazieren.	She goes for a walk in the park.
trinken	to drink
Sie essen und trinken.	They eat and drink.
lachen	to laugh
joggen	to jog
Fußball spielen	to play football, to play soccer
Sie joggen oder spielen Fußball.	They jog or play football.
die Gruppe, -n	group
(das) Yoga	yoga
vorne	ahead, in front
Eine Gruppe macht Yoga und da vorne ist ein Konzert.	A group is doing yoga and there, further ahead, is a concert.

A9 dir (Dat.)	you
Wie geht es dir?	How are you?

der Job, -s	job
mir (Dat.)	I (me)
Mir geht es schlecht.	I'm not doing very well.

A 10 **arbeitslos**	unemployed
gemeinsam	together
etwas	something
gemeinsam etwas tun	to do something together
die Nationalgalerie, -n	national gallery
mitkommen	to come along
Kommst du mit?	Will you come along?
Einverstanden!	Fine.
die Lust	want, desire, wish
Hast du Lust?	Do you want to?

Seite 33

Gespräche im Alltag

der Alltag	everyday life

A 11 die Situation, -en	situation
der Titel, –	title
passen	to fit
Welcher Titel passt?	Which title fits?
sich bedanken	to thank (for something)

einladen	to invite

jemand	someone
ansprechen	to speak to
jemanden ansprechen	to speak to someone
das Befinden	(state of) health
nach dem Befinden fragen	to about one's health

A 12 **ankreuzen**	to mark with a cross
Kreuzen Sie an.	Mark with a cross.
ander-	other
eine andere Situation	an other situation
kennen	to recognize
ihn (Akk.)	him
Sie kennen ihn.	You recognize him.
Ihren (Akk.)	your
Ich weiß Ihren Namen nicht.	I do not know your name.

Wie spät ist es?

spät	late
Wie spät ist es?	What time is it?

A 13 der Vormittag, -e	morning
die Mitternacht	midnight
Mahlzeit!	bon appetit!
halb	half
Es ist halb drei.	It is half past two.
Schlaf gut!	Good night!

Tagesablauf

A 14 die Uhrzeit, -en	time
nehmen	to use, to take
der Bus, -se	bus
den Bus nehmen	to take the bus
die Uni, -s	university
zu Hause sein	to be at home

Beruf

der Beruf, -e	occupation

A 15 die Managerin, -nen	manager
die Bedienung, -en	waiter
der Verkäufer, –	sales person
verdienen	to earn
gut verdienen	to earn well
verkaufen	to sell
die Rechnung, -en	bill, check
studieren	to study
telefonieren	to telephone
das Geschäft, -e	business
Geschäfte machen	to do business
servieren	to serve, to wait on
fahren	to drive
ins Büro fahren	to drive to the office
reisen	to travel
erklären	to explain

die Bestellung, -en	order
Bestellungen notieren	to write down the orders
korrigieren	to correct
Texte korrigieren	to correct texts

5 Essen – Trinken – Einkaufen

Seite 38

Im Bistro

das Bistro, -s	bistro, café, coffee shop

A 1 die Karte, -n	menu
warm	warm
das Getränk, -e	drink
der Tee, -s	tea
die Zitrone, -n	lemon
die Milch	milk
der Espresso, -s	espresso
der Cappuccino, -s	cappuccino
kalt	cold
das Mineralwasser	mineral water
der Orangensaft, "-e	orange juice
der Apfelsaft, "-e	apple juice
die Limonade, -n	lemonade
Cola, das/die, -s	coke
das Ei, -er	egg
das Brötchen, –	roll
die Butter	butter
die Marmelade	marmelade
das Bio-Frühstück	whole-food breakfast
das Müsli, -s	whole-wheat cereal
das Obst	fruit
das/der Joghurt, -s	yoghurt, yogurt
klein	small
die Speise, -n	dish
kleine Speisen	small portions
der Käse	cheese
die Salami, -s	salami
der Schinken	ham

die Mịni-Pizza, -s	mini-pizza
die Tạgessuppe, -n	soup of the day

A2 bestẹllen	to order
nẹhmen	to take, to get for oneself
Ich nehme einen Salat.	I'll take a salad.
kọnnen	may, can
Kann ich auch ein Sand- *wich haben?*	Can I also have a sand-wich?
ạlso	now, we've got . . .

A3 bezạhlen	to pay
stịmmen	to be correct
Stimmt die Rechnung?	Is the bill correct?
mụssen	to have to
Ich muss noch einkaufen.	I still have to go shop-ping.
das Kụrsfest, -e	class party
zạhlen	to pay for
Zahlen, bitte!	We would like to pay, please.

Seite 39

Auf dem Markt

der Mạrkt, "-e	market

A4 bẹide	both
die beiden	both of them
fẹhlen	to miss
Was fehlt noch?	What is still missing?
das Gemụ̈se	vegetable
die Hụ̈hnersuppe	chicken soup
Das Kịlogramm (= kg), –	kilogram
der Spinat	spinach
drạn	to be next
Wer ist dran?	Who is next?
das Hụhn, "-er	chicken
frịsch	fresh
Ist das frisch?	Is it fresh?
schwẹr	heavy
Wie schwer ist das?	How much does it weigh?
das Grạmm (= g), –	gram
nọch eins	another one
Dann brauche ich noch eins.	In that case, I will need another one.

machen	to make, to come to
Das macht dann	That is 12 Euro and
12 Euro fünfzig.	50 cents.
eigentlich	anyhow
Was kochst du eigentlich?	What are you cooking anyhow?
wollen	to want to
die Suppe	soup
Ich will eine Suppe kochen.	I want to make some soup.

A 5 der Einkaufszettel, – shopping list

Einkaufszentrum, Supermarkt, Tante-Emma-Laden

das Einkaufszentrum, -zentren	shopping center/mall
der Supermarkt, "-e	supermarket
der Tante-Emma-Laden, -Läden	corner shop

A 6 die Einkaufsmöglichkeit, -en	shopping opportunities
wenig	little
Die Leute haben wenig Zeit	People have little time.
schnell	short, quickly done
der Fisch, -e	fish
das Fleisch	meat
das Brot, -e	bread
das Milchprodukt, -e	milk product
das Geschäft, -e	store
die Wurst, "-e	sausage (cold cuts)
die Metzgerei, -en	butcher shop
Fleisch und Wurst kann man in der Metzgerei kaufen.	Meats and sausages can be bought at the butcher's.
der Kuchen, –	cake
die Bäckerei, -en	bakery
bekommen	to get
die Lebensmittel	food, groceries
Dort bekommt man auch Lebensmittel.	There, you can also get groceries.
oft	often
teuer	expensive
das Produkt, -e	product
billig	cheap

sonst	anything
Sonst noch etwas?	Anything else?
sofort	right away
Kommt sofort.	I'll be there right away.
kosten	to cost
Das kostet 12 Euro.	That costs 12 Euros.

Seite 40

Das Fest

A 7 die Studentin, -nen	student
der Deutschkurs, -e	German class
feiern	to have a party, to celebrate
Heute feiern sie ein Fest.	Today, they are having a party.
anbieten	to offer
Sie bieten Spezialitäten an.	They offer specialties.
das Sommerfest, -e	summer party
ab	from . . . on
ab 16 Uhr	at 4:00 p.m.
die Sprachenschule, -n	Language School
das Streichquartett, -e	string quartet
das Video, -s	video
das Büfett, -s	buffet
die Disco, -s	discotheque

A 9 dürfen	can
probieren	to try
Darf ich das mal probieren?	Can I try that?
schmecken	to taste
Und, schmeckt's?	And, does it taste good?
das Gericht, -e	dish (food)
Das ist ein Gericht aus Thailand.	This is a dish from Thailand.
scharf	hot, spicy
tanzen	to dance
Ich möchte tanzen.	I want to dance.
verabreden	to make a date
sich verabreden	to make a date with somebody

Seite 41

Nachfragen

| **A 10** die Nudeln (Pl) | noodles, pasta |
| **bedeuten** | to mean |

Was bedeutet „Chicken ...“?	What does "chicken ...." mean?
der Hühnerflügel, –	chicken wing
der Flügel, –	wing
Hm!	Yummy!
prima!	great
drin	in it, in that
Was ist da drin?	What does it consist of?
die Zwiebel, -n	onion
der Sellerie	celery
der Ingwer	ginger

Notizen machen

A 11 das Gewicht, -e	weight
erwarten	to expect
Welche Informationen erwarten Sie?	What information do you expect?
der Pfannkuchen, –	pancake
das Mehl	flour
das Sonderangebot, -e	sale, special offer
der Börsenkurs, -e	stock market rate
die Aktie, -n	stock, share

Seite 42

Lebensmittel

A 12 die Abbildung, -en	picture
der Zucker	sugar
der Reis	rice
der Apfel, "–	apple
die Banane, -n	banana
die Tomate, -n	tomato
der Essig	vinegar
das Öl, -e	oil
das Salz, -e	salt
der Pfeffer	pepper
die Kartoffel, -n	potato

Frühstück, Mittagessen, Abendessen

das Mittagessen, –	lunch
das Abendessen, –	dinner

Studying with pictures and drawings

Pictures and drawings can help your learning. Either draw pictures or cut out illustrations from magazines or catalogues of the vocabulary words you want to remember. Write these words on the edge of the drawings or pictures. If the words are unfamiliar, work with a dictionary. Glue the pictures with their words on a piece of paper or card and look at them regularly.

der Apfel   die Banane

das Brot

Verpackungen

die Verpạckung, -en   packaging

A 14 dies-   these
die Pạckung, -en   carton
die Dọse, -n   can
das Glạs, "-er   glass jar
der Bẹcher, –   cup
die Flạsche, -n   bottle

Write down several words to a topic and while doing so, omit some letters. Later on in the week, complete the word by filling in the missing letters (either orally or written).
Topic: groceries
What are the following words?

Bröt_ _ _ _ ,   Marme_ _ _ _ ,   _ _ _ _ _ _ _ asser ,

_ _ _ üse,   Kä_ _,   _ _ ig,   Sa_ _ _,   Li_ _ _ _ _ _.

Beispiel

Ich möchte/ will Gemüse kochen.

Gemüse kann man auf dem Markt kaufen.

NUDELAUFLAUF MIT GEMÜSE

700 g breite Nudeln
400 g Käse
300 g Tomaten
1/2 kg Spinat
200 g Karotte

Ich muss noch Nudeln kaufen.

6   Sprachen lernen

Seite 46

Lernen: wie und warum?

warum?	why?
Warum lernt Giovanna Deutsch?	Why is Giovanna learning German?

die Apothekerin -nen	pharmacist, druggist
erst	just
erst vier Monate	just four months
der Grund, "-e	reason
ihr-	her
der Österreicher, –	Austrian
Ihr Mann ist Österreicher.	Her husband is Austrian.
zur Zeit	presently, at the moment
jed-	every
Sie lernt jeden Tag Deutsch.	She studies German every day.
besuchen	to attend, to go to

viermal	four times
der Sprachkurs, -e	language class
Viermal pro Woche besucht sie einen Sprachkurs.	She attends a language class four times a week.
der Manager, –	manager
meist	mostly

A 3 der Italienischkurs, -e	Italian class
regelmäßig	regularly
kaum	hardly
das Lehrbuch, "-er	text book
laufen	to be on
Zu Hause läuft oft das Radio.	At home, the radio is often on.

So oder so?

A 4 unterstreichen	underline
Unterstreichen Sie „Ihre" Sätze.	Underline "your" sentences.
vielleicht	perhaps, maybe
folgend-	following
das Ding, -e	thing
Vielleicht machen Sie folgende Dinge gerne.	Perhaps you enjoy doing the following things.
üben	to practice
Aussprache üben	practice pronounciation
die Klasse, -n	class
reden	to speak
Im Kurs reden Sie nicht gerne.	You do not enjoy speaking in class.
der Fehler, –	mistake
der Kollege, -n	colleague
leicht	easy
Sie lernen die Sprache sehr leicht.	You learn the language very easily.
manchmal	sometimes
glauben	to think, to believe
nichts	nothing
Manchmal glauben Sie, Sie lernen nichts genau.	Sometimes you think you are not studying properly.
ein paar	a couple
ein paar Tage	a couple of days
die Übung, -en	exercise

Im Deutschkurs

A 5 das Lernziel, -e — learning objective
der Teilnehmer, – — participant
die Prüfung, -en — exam
mehr — more
Ich möchte mehr Deutsch lernen. — I want to learn more German.
der Sohn, "-e — son
ziemlich — fairly, considerably
Ich kann schon ziemlich viel verstehen. — I can already understand fairly well.
perfekt — perfect
still — quiet
Ich darf nicht immer still sein. — I shouldn't always be so quiet.

A 7 kleben — to paste
das Muster, – — example
Kleben Sie Sätze nach dem Muster. — Paste sentences according to the example.
ausschneiden — to cut out
gehören — to go with, to belong to
Die Sätze gehören zu einem Bild. — The sentences belong to a picture.
korrekt — correctly
weiterhelfen — to help along, to assist
die Lehrerin, -nen — teacher
Die Lehrerin hilft weiter. — The teacher helps along.
das Blatt, "-er — page
zeigen — to show
die Kollegin, -nen — colleague
zweimal — two times
aufnehmen — to record
die Kassette, -n — tape
Ich nehme etwas auf Kassette auf. — I record things on tape.

Lerntipps

der Lerntipp, -s — learning tip

A 8 aufpassen	to pay attention to
der Unterricht	class
Ich passe im Unterricht gut auf.	I pay attention in class.
die Tandem-Partnerin, -nen	tandem partner
neu	again
Ich schreibe zu Hause alles neu.	I rewrite everything at home.
wiederholen	to reiterate, to go over again
schwer	difficult
mich (Akk.)	me
Die Grammatik ist für mich nicht schwer.	Grammar is not difficult for me.
die Mediothek, -en	mediathek

A 10 der Tipp, -s	suggestion
der Plan, "-e	plan
das Beispiel, -e	example
immer	always
testen	to test
dich (Akk.)	you
selbst	one's own self
Teste dich selbst.	Test yourself.

Tip

Study Methods

Plan your method of studying. Write a list in your calendar: what you want to learn, how you want to learn, how much time to spend studying, when to review. Complete the tests and review the things you do not know for sure.

What do I want to learn?	How shall I study?	Time	Review
Verbs in the Present	Xerox copy A1 to the text on p. 46 and omit the endings	15 minutes	in three days
The Accusative Case with its corresponding article	Write down 10 objects Speak out loud: *Das ist **ein** Stift. – Ich habe **einen** Stift.*	15 minutes	

kontroll<u>ie</u>ren	to control, check, verify
Kontrollieren Sie Ihr	Do you check your study-
Lernen?	ing?

Seite 49

Texte verstehen: auf wichtige Wörter achten

A 12 str<u>ei</u>chen	to take off the list
Warum ist Nobuhiko	Why is Nobuhiko taken
gestrichen?	off the list?
die L<u>e</u>rnpartnerin, -en	study partner

E-Mails schicken

A 13 s<u>e</u>nden	to send
Sie wollen eine E-Mail	You want to send an
senden.	email.
st<u>a</u>rten	to start
das Programm starten	to start the program
Sie starten das Programm.	Start the program.
der Bef<u>e</u>hl, -e	command
die Adr<u>e</u>ssliste, -n	list of addresses
das Comp<u>u</u>terwort, "-er	computer word
sp<u>ei</u>chern	to store
dr<u>u</u>cken	to print out
l<u>ö</u>schen	to delete
sch<u>i</u>cken	to send, to mail
Schick mir bitte mehr	Send me more words
Wörter.	please.

Seite 50

Im Kursraum

der K<u>u</u>rsraum, "-e	classroom

A 15 das W<u>ö</u>rterbuch,"-er	dictionary
der T<u>i</u>sch, -e	table
der St<u>u</u>hl, "-e	chair
das Pap<u>ie</u>r	paper
der St<u>i</u>ft, -e	pencil
der K<u>u</u>gelschreiber, –	ball-point pen
das Etu<u>i</u>, -s	pencil case
die T<u>a</u>fel, -n	board

die Landkarte, -n	map
der Recorder, –	tape recorder
der CD-Player, –	CD player
die CD-ROM, -s	CD-ROM

Lernen mit der CD-ROM

A 16 der Ausdruck, "-e	expression
einlegen	to place in
Legen Sie die CD-ROM in den Computer ein.	Place the CD-ROM in the computer.
das Lernprogramm, -e	study program
anklicken	to click on
das Kapitel, –	chapter
Klicken Sie das Kapitel an.	Click on the chapter.
auswählen	to choose
drücken	to push
Wählen Sie eine Übung aus und drücken Sie „Play".	Choose an exercise and push "play".
nächst-	next
Gehen Sie zur nächsten Übung.	Go to the next exercise.
die Lösung, -en	answer
die Hilfe, -n	help, assistance

Tip

Say it in German.

Repeat the current patterns you are learning in German out loud.

die Dat**ei**, -en	data file
be**e**nden	to close
Beenden Sie das Programm.	Close the program.

Seite 54

Ferien an der Nordsee

die F**e**rien (Pl)	holiday, vacation
die N**o**rdsee	North Sea
A 1 die R**ei**se, –	trip, journey
der Z**u**g, "-e	train
Ich bin mit dem Zug gereist.	I came by train.
f**a**st	about
w**a**rten	to wait (for)
Ich habe zwei Stunden gewartet.	I waited two hours.
über**a**ll	everywhere
die SMS, –	short-message, SMS
w**ei**terfahren	to continue, to travel on
Ich bin dann weitergefahren.	I then continued my trip.
das M**ee**r, -e	ocean
b**u**chen	to book
Wir haben hier ein Hotel gebucht.	We booked a hotel here.
gem**ü**tlich	relaxing, comfortable
die **Au**ssicht	view
phant**a**stisch	fantastic
der H**i**mmel	sky
endlos	endless
w**ei**t	extensive
Der Himmel und das Meer sind endlos weit.	The sky and ocean are endlessly extensive.
der St**au**, -s	traffic jam
der Fl**u**ghafen, "–	airport
sch**a**de	too bad, how unfortunate

A2 die Station, "-en	stop, place	
das Verkehrsmittel, –	form of transportation	

A3 endlich	finally, at last
der Spaziergang, "-e	walk
stundenlang	for hours
laufen	to walk
Man kann stundenlang am Strand laufen.	You can walk on the beach for hours.
der Strand, "-e	beach
der Sand	sand
die Welle, -n	waves
der Horizont	horizon
der Leuchtturm, "-e	light house
berühmt	famous, well-known
dorthin	there
wandern	to walk
Dorthin sind wir dann gewandert.	There is where we then walked.
der Tourist, -en	tourist
uns (Akk.)	us
euch (Akk.)	you
fotografieren	to take a picture of
Soll ich euch fotografieren?	Shall I take your picture?
das Restaurant, -s	restaurant
der Deich, -e	dike
lecker	delicious
zurückfahren	to ride back, to drive, to return
Am Abend sind wir zurückgefahren.	In the evening we drove back.

A4 das Vergangene	past (events)
berichten	to tell about
über Vergangenes berichten	tell about past events

Seite 55

Ausflug nach Seebüll

der Ausflug, "-e	excursion

A5 die Karte, -n	map
nahe	near
an	to

die Grenze, -n	border
nahe an der Grenze	near the border
der Maler, –	painter, artist
das Auto, -s	car
mieten	to rent
falsch	wrong
Dort ist Robert falsch	That is where Robert drove
gefahren.	in the wrong direction.
breit	wide
weit und breit	far and wide
der Friese, -n	a native Frieslander
Plattdeutsch	Low German
das Haus, "-er	building
der Garten, "–	garden
so wie	just like, just as
früher	in the past
so wie früher	just as in the past
der Museumsshop, -s	museum shop
der Katalog, -e	catalogue
das Geschenk, -e	gift, present
der Kilometer (= km), –	kilometer
traurig	sad

Tip

Repeat grammar rules through examples

Copy a sentence from your textbook or make a note of a few sentences from a specific chapter. For example, from this chapter: *Was haben Sie gestern oder am Wochenende gemacht?* Write down the grammar terms for the sentence and specify where they belong.

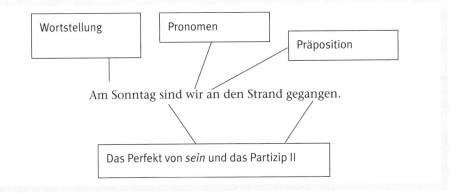

A 7 der Hauptbahn-	main train station
hof, "-e	
das Taxi, -s	taxi
helfen	to help
Können Sie uns helfen?	Can you help us?
zweit-	second
die zweite Straße links	the second street on the left
vor Klanxbüll	before Klanxbüll
meinen	to mean
Wie meinen Sie das?	What do you mean by that?
die Kreuzung, -en	crossing

Seite 56

Die Rückfahrt

die Rückfahrt, -en	return trip

A 8 die Durchsage, -n	announcement
frei	free, not occupied
Entschuldigung, ist hier noch frei?	Excuse me, is this seat free?
wegnehmen	to remove

die Tasche, -n	bag
Ich nehme die Tasche weg.	I'll take my bag away.
lassen	to leave
Nein, bitte lassen Sie sie da.	No, please leave it there.
freundlich	nice, polite
rauchen	to smoke
Darf man hier rauchen?	Is smoking allowed here?
der Nichtraucher, –	non-smoker
(= das Nichtraucherab-	
teil, -e)	

Tip

Practice role playing together.

Which situation would you like to act out?   **Im Zug**
Collect the necessary sentences and expressions.
Act out the situation.

Entschuldigung, ist hier noch frei?

die F**a**hrkarte, -n	ticket
die B**a**hncard, -s	train pass
Ah, h**ie**r!	Oh, here you are.
entsch**u**ldigen	to excuse
Entschuldigen Sie!	Excuse me!

A 9 die **A**bfahrt, -en	departure
das Glei**s, -e**	track

A 10 s**i**cher	for sure, certainly
Ja, sicher.	Yes, for sure.
der W**a**gen, –	car
die Versp**ä**tung, -en	delay
Hat der Zug Verspätung?	Is the train delayed?
p**ü**nktlich	on time, punctual
der Pa**ss, "-e**	passport
ger**a**de	just
Ich habe den Pass gerade	I just had my passport in
noch gehabt.	my hand.

Seite 57

Ein Miniglossar benutzen

das M**i**niglossar, -e	mini-glossary
ben**u**tzen	to use
ein Miniglossar benutzen	to use a mini-glossary

A 11 reserv**ie**ren	to reserve
le**tzt-**	last
Ich habe letzte Woche	I reserved a room last
ein Zimmer reserviert.	week.

A 12 das WC, -s	bathroom
der Balko**n, -e**	balcony
das TV (= Fernsehen)	television
die M**i**nibar, -s	mini-bar
zentr**a**l	central
die L**a**ge	location
zentrale Lage	central location
die Pensi**o**n, -en	bed and breakfast
der S**ee**blick	seaview, lakeview
der St**a**dtrand, "-er	outskirts of the city
ru**hig**	quiet
der See**, -n**	lake

Schöne Ferien!

Study words in relation to each other.

A 14	der Sommer, –	summer
	planen	to plan
	die Ferien planen	to plan the holiday
	festlegen	to set
	das Datum festlegen	to set the date
	das Reisebüro, -s	travel office

Learn nouns and verbs in phrases, together. It is possible to learn a good number of nouns and verbs that way.

die Idee, -n	idea
der Fahrplan, "-e	schedule
(das) Tennis	tennis
Tennis spielen	*to play tennis*
wechseln	to exchange
Geld wechseln	to exchange money
baden	to swim
im Meer baden	to swim in the ocean
die Karte, -n	ticket

Musik – hören
Gitarre – spielen
Hotel – buchen
Auto – fahren . . .

Gute Reise!

A 15	der Flug, "-e	flight
	der Schalter, –	counter
	umsteigen	to change, to transfer

Learn the verbs and their past participles

Study with cards: write the infinitive on one side and the past participle on the other side. Learn both forms. Use the past participle in a sentence out loud, such as:
Gestern habe ich . . . / Gestern bin ich . . .

fragen	gefragt	zeigen	gezeigt
sehen	gesehen	fahren	gefahren

die Haltestelle, -n	stop
landen	to land
die Straßenbahn, -en	tram
einsteigen	to enter
die Autobahn, -en	highway, motorway
das Schiff, -e	boat, ship
der Parkplatz, "-e	parking place
parken	to park
der Bahnsteig, -e	platform
abholen	to pick up
der Hafen, "–	harbour
die Fahrt, -en	trip, journey
das Fahrrad, "-er	bicycle
die Ampel, -n	traffic light
das Flugzeug, -e	airplane

8 Wohnen

Seite 62

Turmwohnung

die Turmwohnung, -en	an apartment in a tower
A1 die Wohn-situation, -en	living situation
die Wohnung, -en	apartment, flat
der Turm, "-e	tower
der Turmwächter, –	tower watchman
die Frau (= Ehefrau), -en	wife
hoch	high
oben	up
auf die Höhe, -n	at the height of
etwa auf 50 Meter Höhe	about 50 meters high
groß	large
War die Wohnung nicht zu groß?	Wasn't the apartment too large?
wie viel ?	how many?
viel-	many
das Wohnzimmer, –	living room

das Schlafzimmer, –	bedroom
die Küche, -n	kitchen
der Stock, Stockwerke	floor, story
im zweiten Stock	on the second floor
doch	yes, of course
rund	round
um	about
rund um die Wohnung	round about the apartment
besonders	special, unique
Die Aussicht war ganz besonders.	The view was something special.
das Wetter	weather
sogar	even
die Alpen (Pl)	Alps
sicher	for sure
Das war sicher toll	That must have been terrific.
der Münsterturm, "-e	Münster Tower
der Aussichtspunkt, -e	observation point

A3 **der Raum**, "-e   room

Seite 63

Wohnen in Bern

A4 die Geschichte	history
das Wappentier, -e	heraldic animal
der Bär, -en	bear
der Bärengraben	bear burrow – a tourist attraction in Bern, a trench with live bears
der Fluss, "-e	river
aufwachsen	to grow up
Er ist in Bern aufgewachsen.	He grew up in Bern.
die Hauptstadt, "-e	capital
die Region, -en	region

A5 **geboren sein**	to be born
Sie ist in Spanien geboren.	She was born in Spain.
mit zwölf Jahren	at the age of twelve
die Miete, -n	rent
viel Miete bezahlen	to pay a high rent
der Stadtmensch, -en	city person

<u>au</u>sgehen	to go out
Sie ist oft ausgegangen.	She went out often.
h<u>eu</u>te	now
das L<u>a</u>nd	country
Sie wohnt auf dem Land.	Now she lives in the country.
das B<u>au</u>ernhaus, "-er	country house, farm house
die R<u>u</u>he	peace and quiet
Sie hat gern Ruhe.	She likes her peace and quiet.
das D<u>o</u>rf, "-er	village
der W<u>o</u>hnblock, "-e	apartment house
s<u>ei</u>n-	his
die Fr<u>eu</u>ndin	girlfriend
(= Partnerin), **-nen**	
die Einz<u>i</u>mmer-	one-room apartment
wohnung, -en	
w<u>e</u>ggehen	to leave
Sie ist mit 16 weggegangen.	At 16, she left home.
die Fabr<u>i</u>k, -en	factory
h<u>ei</u>raten	to marry, to get married
Vor zehn Jahren hat sie geheiratet.	She got married ten years ago.
gesch<u>ie</u>den sein	to be divorced
Heute ist sie geschieden.	Now she is divorced.
das K<u>i</u>nd, -er	child
vor k<u>u</u>rzem	just recently
<u>u</u>mziehen	to move
Sie ist vor kurzem umgezogen.	She moved just recently.
die S<u>ie</u>dlung, -en	housing estate
mod<u>e</u>rn	modern
pr<u>a</u>ktisch	practical
komfort<u>a</u>bel	comfortable

A 6 die N<u>ä</u>he	vicinity
in der Nähe von Hamburg	close to Hamburg
die M<u>a</u>lerin, -nen	painter, artist
der Quadr<u>a</u>tmeter (= qm), –	square meter
br<u>ei</u>t	wide
l<u>a</u>ng	long
3 Meter lang und 4 Meter breit	3 meters long and 4 meters wide

In der Siedlung

A 7 der W<u>o</u>hnraum, "-e	living area
die M<u>ö</u>bel (Pl)	furniture
dr<u>au</u>ßen	outside
Die Kinder können draußen spielen.	The children can play outside.
die S-Bahn, -en	train
der N<u>a</u>chbar, -n	neighbor
der/die Bek<u>a</u>nnte, -n	acquaintance
origin<u>e</u>ll	unconventional, original
sch<u>o</u>n	sure enough, certainly
Mir gefällt es schon.	I certainly like it.
das S<u>o</u>fa, -s	sofa
bl<u>au</u>	blue
ov<u>a</u>l	oval
der S<u>e</u>ssel, –	arm chair
gr<u>ü</u>n	green
die W<u>a</u>nd, "-e	wall
g<u>e</u>lb	yellow
zus<u>a</u>mmenpassen	to go together
Das passt nicht zusammen.	It doesn't go together.
der B<u>o</u>den, –	floor
gr<u>au</u>	gray
der T<u>e</u>ppich, -e	carpet, rug
r<u>o</u>sa	pink
daz<u>u</u>	in addition to
aus H<u>o</u>lz	out of wood, wooden
das H<u>o</u>lz, "-er	wood
die L<u>a</u>mpe, -n	lamp
h<u>i</u>nten	back
das Bild da hinten	the painting back there
w<u>o</u>hl	(wonder) whether
Wo ist das wohl?	I wonder whether you know where this is?
das F<u>i</u>lm-Foto, -s	photograph from a film / movie
der H<u>e</u>rd, -e	stove
der Kn<u>o</u>pf, "-e	button
die H<u>ei</u>zung, -en	heating system
das G<u>a</u>s, -e	gas
das <u>Ö</u>l, -e	oil
h<u>ei</u>zen	to heat

Früher haben wir mit Öl geheizt.	We used to heat with oil.
die Toilette, -n	bathroom
wirklich	really
Schön, wirklich schön.	Very nice really, very nice.
gratulieren	to congratulate
Gratuliere!	Congratulations!
(= Ich gratuliere Ihnen.)	(I congratulate you.)
das Kinderzimmer, –	nursery
der Schreibtisch, -e	desk
das Bücherregal, -e	book case
gleich	just
Da ist gleich die Autobahn.	The highway is just over there.
laut	loud

A 8 der Gegenstand, "-e object

Seite 65

Ein Bild beschreiben

Tip

Put a file together, collect your own texts.

Collect your own printed matter, make sure it is correct. Mark the expressions and phrases you find interesting and use them, when appropriate, in writing new German texts.

A 10 der Kommentar, -e	commentary
die Villa, -en	villa, stately home
der Hügel, –	hill
nennen	to call
Sie hat es „Villen am Hügel" genannt.	She called it "Villas on the Hill".
das Fenster, –	window
schwarz	black
das Dach, "-er	roof
rostbraun	rust brown
hellgelb	light yellow
durch	across
gehen	to go
die Linie, -n	line
Durch das Bild geht eine Linie.	A line goes across the painting.
oben	above
unten	below
malen	to paint
Sie hat den Himmel grün gemalt.	She painted the sky green.
schräg	tilted

Die Häuser stehen schräg auf dem Hügel.	The houses on the hill are tilted.
vorne	in front
die Pflanze, -n	plant
der Baum, "-e	tree
einfach	simple
primitiv	primitive
leer	bare
Das Bild ist leer	The painting is bare.

Seite 66

Farben, Möbel und Gegenstände

A 13		
der Spiegel, –	mirror
der Schrank, "-e	cupboard
der Fernseher, –	television
das Regal, -e	shelf
das Kissen, –	pillow
weiß	white
braun	brown
rot	red
orange	orange
violett	violet

Räume und Häuser

A 14	
hineinschreiben	to fill in
Schreiben Sie die Wörter hinein.	Fill in the words.
die Anzahl	number (of)
der Keller, –	cellar

Tip

Say it in the past

The perfect tense is usually used in German when telling a story or past experience. When using the verbs *sein* and *haben* and auxiliary modals, the past tense is then used since this form is shorter.

wohnen	(Perfekt)	Ich habe in Berlin gewohnt.
haben	(Präteritum)	Ich hatte ein Zimmer.
sein	(Präteritum)	Das war in einem Studentenheim.

| die Decke, -n | ceiling |
| die Treppe, -n | stairway |

| das Erdgeschoss, -e | first floor, ground floor |
| der Kamin, -e | chimney |

9 | Einladen – Kochen – Essen

Seite 70

Die Einladung

| die Einladung, -en | invitation |

| **A 1** der Arbeits-
kollege, -n | colleague |

A 3 empfangen	to receive
dass	that
Schön, dass Sie kommen.	How nice of you to have come.
mitbringen	to bring
Das habe ich Ihnen mitgebracht.	I brought this for you.
die Blume, -n	flower
freuen	to please
Freut mich.	Pleased to meet you.
der Aperitif, -s	aperitif, before-dinner drink
der Sekt	sparkling wine
das Bier, -e	beer
der Wein, -e	wine
der Saft, "-e	juice
das Wohl	health
Zum Wohl!	To your health!
dein-	your
der Freund (= Partner), -e	boy friend
der Chef, -s	boss
persönlich	personally
Heute kocht der Chef persönlich.	Today the boss is cooking personally.
bringen	to bring
ihm (Dat.)	him

Wir bringen ihm auch einen Sekt.	Let's bring him a sparkling wine too.

A4 erleben
Was haben Sie erlebt?

to experience
What did you experience?

Seite 71

Die Speisekarte

die Speisekarte, -n	menu
anbrennen	to burn
Das Essen ist angebrannt	The food was burnt.

A5 zusammenstellen — to put together, to combine

das Menü, -s	menu
Stellen Sie ein Menü zusammen.	Put a menu together.
die Vorspeise, -n	hors d'oeuvre, appetizer
die Hauptspeise, -n	entree, main dish

A6 geschehen
Was geschieht?
klingen

to happen
What happens?
to sound

Tip

Classify words according to ideas or concepts

Write down the names for different foods which are of interest to you. Put these words in groups, according to headings. It is easier to remember different words if they belong to the same category. Avoid large word groups, at best ca. 7 words.
Make a note also of your favorite foods as well as food which is important to you:

Ich darf keinen Spinat essen.

Suppe,
Filet,
Forelle,
Eis,
Torte,
Schnitzel,
Reis . . .

Vorspeisen	Hauptspeisen	Nachtisch
Suppe	Filet	

Das klingt gut.	That sounds good.
riesengroß	huge
der Hunger	hunger
Ich habe so einen Hunger!	I am so hungry!
vegetarisch	vegetarian
Gibt es auch Vegetarisches?	Are there vegetarian dishes also?
bestimmt	definitely
Es gibt bestimmt noch mehr ohne Fleisch.	There are definitely more meatless dishes.
reingehen	to go in, to enter
Gehen wir doch einfach rein.	Let's just go inside.
hoffen	to hope
Ich hoffe, es ist noch Platz.	I hope there is room.
überreichen	to present
ein Geschenk überreichen	to present a gift
lieb	nice
Das ist aber lieb von dir.	That is so nice of you.

Seite 72

Imbiss

der Imbiss, -e	snack

A 8 worüber?	about what
Worüber sprechen sie?	What are they talking about?
besser	better
nie	never
Du bist nie zufrieden.	You are never satisfied.
der Superkoch, "-e	master cook
der Döner, –	döner
fein	good
Sehr fein!	Very good!
Alles Gute!	Wish you the best!
Auf dich!	Here's to you!

A 9 der Smalltalk	small talk, chitchat

A 10 die Postkarte, -n	postcard
Liebe Petra, . . .	Dear Petra, . . .
der Dönerstand, "-e	döner stand
richtig	really
Das war richtig gut!	That was really good!
der Blumenstrauß, "-e	bouquet of flowers

schenken	to give
der Appetit	appetite
Guten Appetit!	Bon appetit!
Prost!	Cheers!
versuchen	to try
Möchtest du mal versuchen?	Would you like to try this?

Seite 73

Texte kürzen

kürzen	to shorten
Texte kürzen	to shorten texts

A 11 die Zutat, -en	ingredient
die Zeichnung, -en	drawing
der Auflauf, "-e	casserole
die Karotte, -n	carrot
gießen	to pour, to add . . . to
Milch dazu gießen	to add milk to
rühren	to stir
alles gut rühren	to stir everything well
die Sauce, -n	sauce
würzen	to spice, to season
mit Salz und Pfeffer würzen	to season with salt and pepper
schneiden	to cut
den Käse in Scheiben schneiden	to cut the cheese in slices
schälen	to peel
die Tomaten schälen	to peel tomatoes
ca. (= circa)	around, about
der Backofen, "–	oven
einschalten	to turn on
den Backofen auf 180 °C einschalten	to turn the oven on to 180 °C

A 13 der Textbaustein, -e	text building blocks
der Vegetarier, –	vegetarian
die Torte, -n	cake, layer cake
gesund	healthy
Ich esse sehr gesund.	I eat healthy food.
kalt	cold
Am Abend esse ich gerne kalt.	I like to eat cold dishes in the evening.

genießen	to enjoy
Ich genieße das.	I enjoy it.
als	than
Das mag ich lieber als zu Mittag essen.	I like that better than eating in at lunchtime.

Seite 74

Kochen und essen

A 15 der Durst	thirst
Durst haben	to be thirsty
waschen	to wash
den Salat waschen	to wash the lettuce
decken	to set
den Tisch decken	to set the table
satt	full
satt sein	to have had enough
abräumen	to clear
den Tisch abräumen	to clear the table
das Geschirr	dishes
abwaschen	to wash
das Geschirr abwaschen	to wash the dishes

Den Tisch decken

A 16 der Topf, "-e	pot
die Schüssel, -n	bowl
die Tasse, -n	cup
die Serviette, -n	napkin
die Gabel, -n	fork
der Teller, –	dish
der Löffel, –	spoon
das Messer, –	knife

Was ist . . .?

A 7 süß	sweet
sauer	bitter
trocken	dry
heiß	hot
das Eis	ice cream

Seite 75

| **die Sahne** | cream |
| der Obstsalat, -e | fruit salad |

Tip

Draw Words – Drawing with Words

You usually know where and what there is to eat on a table. It is much easier to remember these words visually. Make a drawing of a set table.
Repeat by drawing an empty table and "set it" by writing in the appropriate words.

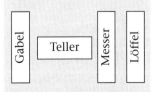

worauf?   to what?
Worauf beziehen sich die   What do the words refer
  Wörter?   to?

10   Körper und Gesundheit

der Körper, –   body
die Gesundheit / e   health

Krank → Krankleit = enfermo.

Du musst zum Arzt

der Arzt, "-e   doctor

A 1 die Krankheit, -en   sickness, illness
aussehen   to look, to appear
Du siehst schlecht aus.   You look terrible.
los sein   to be the matter
Was ist los mit dir?   What is wrong with you?
der Hals, "-e   throat
weh   to be sore
Mein Hals tut weh.   I have a sore throat.
hinlegen   to lay down
Willst du dich nicht hinlegen? Don't you think you
                                   should be in bed?

vorbeigehen   to pass
Das geht vorbei.   This will pass.
die Schmerztablette, -n   painkiller
nehmen   to take
Ich habe schon eine Schmerz-   I already took a pain killer.
  tablette genommen.
zu viel   too much

A 2 **krank**   sick
Er war krank.   He was sick.
konzentrieren (sich)   to concentrate
Er konnte sich nicht   He could not concentrate.
  konzentrieren.

Tip

Take breaks while studying.

- Do not study too much at once.
- Study for 30 minutes, then take a 5 minute break. (Stand up, open the window, drink a glass of water, move around.)
- Then start studying again for another 30 minutes.
- Taking breaks is just as important as study time.

die Kopfschmerzen (Pl)	headache
anrufen	to call
Er hat den Arzt angerufen.	He called the doctor.
die Anmeldung, -en	office
die Versicherungskarte, -n	health insurance card
das Wartezimmer, –	waiting room
setzen (sich)	to sit down
Er hat sich ins Warte-	He sat in the waiting
zimmer gesetzt.	room.

A3 fühlen	to feel
schwach	weak
Ich fühle mich schwach.	I feel weak.
das Fieber	temperature
messen	to take, to measure
Ich habe noch nicht Fieber	I haven't taken my
gemessen.	temperature yet.
der Schmerz, -en	pain
genau	exactly
Wo tut es genau weh?	Where does it hurt
	exactly?
vor allem	mainly, principally
der Arm, -e	arm
das Bein, -e	leg
gestern	yesterday
tief	deep
einatmen	to breathe in, to inhale
bitte tief einatmen	breathe in deeply, please
ausatmen	to exhale
und jetzt ausatmen	and now exhale

Seite 79

Gute Besserung . . .

die Besserung	improvement
Gute Besserung!	Gett well soon!

A4 die Anleitung, -en	direction
wogegen?	against what?
wie oft?	how often?
verwenden	to use, to apply
Wie verwenden Sie	How should OptiCitran be
OptiCitran?	used?

auflösen	to dissolve
der Bedarf	need
wiederholen	to repeat
bei Bedarf wiederholen	repeat if needed
die Tageszeit	time of day
einnehmen	to take
Sie können OptiCitran zu	OptiCitran can be taken
jeder Tageszeit einnehmen.	throughout the day.
beachten	to be cautious of
zu (+ Infinitiv)	to
Was ist zu beachten?	What should I be cautious of?
die Erkältung	cold
bei Beginn der Erkältung	to take at the start of a
einnehmen	cold
die Grippe	flu
der Schnupfen	sniffles, cold
die Halsschmerzen (Pl)	sore throat
die Gliederschmerzen (Pl)	muscle ache
das Vitamin, -e	vitamine
Heißgetränk mit Vitamin C	hot drink with vitamine C
A 5 der Arztbesuch, -e	doctor's visit
das Rezept, -e	prescription
die Apotheke, -en	pharmacist
das Medikament, -e	medication
das Bett, -en	bed
legen	to lie down
Er hat sich ins Bett gelegt.	He went to bed.
vorbei sein	to be gone
Nach ein paar Tagen war	After a few days, the fever
das Fieber vorbei.	was gone.
A 6 die Auskunft, "-e	information
geben	to give out
Auskunft geben	to give out information
worum?	about what?
Worum geht es?	What is it about?
das Halsweh	sore throat
das Kopfweh	headache
völlig	completely
kaputt	exhausted

Ich war völlig kaputt.	I was completely exhausted.
liegen	to lie
Jetzt liege ich im Bett.	Right now, I'm lying in bed.
der Honig	honey

A7 erkältet sein — to have a cold, to be sick
Sie sind erkältet. — You have got a cold.

Seite 80

Ein Arzt gibt Auskunft

A8 **Dr. (= der Doktor, -en)** — Dr., doctor

zwischen	between
der Patient, -en	patient
das Gespräch zwischen Arzt und Patient	the conversation between the doctor and patient
die Checkliste, -n	check list
sondern	but
zuhören	to listen to
wenn	if
Als Arzt muss man gut zuhören.	As a good doctor, one has to be a good listener.
die Hand, "-e	hand
der Fuß, "-e	foot
Er redet mit Händen und Füßen.	He speaks with his hands and feet.
häufig	frequent
häufige Krankheiten	frequent sicknesses / ailments
die Angst, "-e	fear
der Erwachsene, -n	adult
die Rückenschmerzen (Pl)	back pain
genug	enough
die Bewegung, -en	exercise
Die Leute haben nicht genug Bewegung.	People do not get enough exercise.
sitzen	to sit
Sie sitzen zu lange vor dem Fernseher.	They sit in front of the television too long.
der/die Jugendliche, -n	young person, youth
verletzen (sich)	to injure oneself

> **Tip**
>
> **Learn clauses.**
>
> In an *if*-clause the verb is always at the end of the sentence. The *if*-clause can appear before or after the main clause. Note a few important clauses on cards.
> On the front of the card, put the *if*-clause after the main clause.
> On the back of the card, put the if-clause in front of the main clause.
>
> Ich komme gern, **wenn** ich Zeit habe.
>
> **Wenn** ich Zeit habe, komme ich gern.

Jugendliche verletzen sich beim Sport.	Young people injure themselves in sports.
die Sportverletzung, -en	sports injury
die Verstauchung, -en	sprain
die Schnittwunde, -n	deep cut
der Sportunfall, "-e	sports accident
brechen	to break
Sie brechen sich einen Fuß.	They break a foot.
das Krankenhaus, "-er	hospital
die Luft	air
Kleine Kinder haben oft Probleme mit der schlechten Luft.	Small children often have problems with air pollution.
der Husten	cough
die Ohrenschmerzen (Pl)	earache

A 9 stellen	to ask
Welche Fragen stellt der Arzt?	What questions does the doctor ask?
der Arbeitgeber, –	employer
der Allgemeinzustand	general condition
die Verdauung	digestion
der Schlaf	sleep
das Herz, -en	heart
die Atmung	respiration
die Haut	skin
das Auge, -n	eye

A 10 das Stichwort, -er	heading
beantworten	to answer
Beantworten Sie die Fragen.	Answer the questions.
aufwachen	to wake up
Wachen Sie in der Nacht oft auf?	Do you often wake up at night?
das Einschlafen	falling asleep
Probleme beim Einschlafen	having problems falling asleep
funktionieren	to function
Funktioniert die Verdauung?	Does the digestive system function properly?
die Zigarette, -n	cigarette
treiben	to practice
Treiben Sie Sport?	Do you practice sports?
das Asthma	asthma

Lernen mit Bewegung

A 11 **mịtmachen** — to join in, to follow suit
Machen Sie mit. — Join in.
die Fịtness-Übung, -en — fitness exercise
die Übung, -en — exercise
vọrspielen — to demonstrate
Spielen Sie vor. — Demonstrate.
gegen — for, to help
Übungen gegen Rücken- — Exercises against back-
schmerzen — aches
stẹllen — to stand
hịnter — behind
Stellen Sie sich hinter den — Stand behind the chair.
Stuhl.
der Rụcken — back
gerạde — straight
Der Rücken ist gerade. — The back is straight.
legen — to place, to put
Legen Sie die Hände auf — Place your hands on the
den Stuhl. — chair.
gehen — to bend down
das Knie, – — knee
Gehen Sie jetzt in die Knie. — Now bend your knees.
liegen — to be on
Die Hände liegen auf — The hands are on the
dem Stuhl. — chair.
aufstehen — to stand up
Und jetzt stehen Sie wieder — And now, stand up again.
auf.
atmen — to breathe
Und dazu regelmäßig atmen. — While doing this, breathe
— regularly.
entspạnnen — to relax
Die Beine sind entspannt. — Legs are relaxed.

Lernkärtchen

das Lẹrnkärtchen, – — study card

A 12 der Beịspielsatz, "-e — an example sentence

> **Tip**
>
> **Studying Problems**
>
> It is very usual to have problems in learning new things. Some topics are easily forgotten or were never properly understood. A good suggestion as to how to solve these problems is: write the problem words and sentences on a piece of paper; hang this paper up somewhere where you see it often (for example, on the entrance door, by the window, on the fridge . . .); when you come across this problem again, just read your paper through.

Körper und Gesicht

das Gesicht, -er	face

A 13 verbinden	to connect
die Figur, -en	figure
Verbinden Sie die Wörter mit der Figur.	Connect the words to the figure.
halblaut	whisper out loud
der Kreis, -e	circle
das Haar, -e ————	hair
der Zahn, "-e	tooth
das Ohr, -en	ear
die Lippe, -n	lip
der Mund, "-er	mouth
die Nase, -n	nose
✗ **der Kopf, "-e** ————	head ——→
die Brust, "-e	chest
der Bauch, "-e	stomach
der Finger, –	finger

Tätigkeiten

die Tätigkeit, -en	activity

A 14 anfassen	to touch, to hold
tragen	to carry
putzen	to clean
zumachen	to close
aufmachen	to open
küssen	to kiss
husten	to cough
riechen	to smell
springen	to jump

→ *die Verse / der Hacke → tobillo.*
→ *der Rücken*
↳ *der Hals → cuello*
↳ *die Schulter /n → hombros*
der Rücken - espalda
der Daumen → pulgar. / daumen en pl.

die Kl<u>ei</u>dung | clothing

Kleider machen Leute

die Kl<u>ei</u>der (Pl)	clothes
m<u>a</u>chen	to make
Kleider machen Leute.	Clothes make the man.

A 1 das Kl<u>ei</u>dungsstück, -e	piece of clothing
sort<u>ie</u>ren	to sort out
Sortieren Sie die Kleidungsstücke.	Sort out the clothing.
der El<u>e</u>ktriker, –	electrician
<u>a</u>nziehen (sich)	to dress in
sp<u>o</u>rtlich	casual
Ich ziehe mich sportlich an.	I dress casually.
die J<u>ea</u>ns, –	jeans
bequ<u>e</u>m	comfortable
Ich mag bequeme Kleidung.	I like comfortable clothes.
s<u>au</u>ber	clean
<u>o</u>rdentlich	in order, in good condition
der <u>A</u>nzug, "-e	suit
s<u>e</u>lten	seldom, hardly ever
Anzüge trage ich selten.	I hardly ever wear suits.
die Sp<u>o</u>rtkleidung	sports clothes
der J<u>o</u>gginganzug, "-e	jogging suit
das T-Shirt, -s	t-shirt
der T<u>u</u>rnschuh, -e	tennis shoe, trainer, sneaker
die Gesch<u>ä</u>ftsfrau, -en	business woman
der R<u>o</u>ck, "-e	skirt
sch<u>i</u>ck	fashionable, smart
die Bl<u>u</u>se, -n	blouse
die J<u>a</u>cke, -n	jacket
l<u>ä</u>ssig	informal
Das ist mir zu lässig.	That is too informal for me.
m<u>o</u>disch	stylish
das Kl<u>ei</u>d, -er	dress

ausgeben	to spend
Ich gebe nicht viel Geld für Kleidung aus.	I do not spend much money on clothes.
das Sonderangebot, -e	special offer
die Regenjacke, -n	rain jacket
der Mantel, "–	coat
der Second-Hand-Laden, "–	second-hand shop
die Mode	fashion
der Quatsch	nonsense
So ein Quatsch!	That is complete nonsense!
die Ärztin, -nen	doctor, physician
die Berufskleidung	professional clothes
die Freizeitkleidung	leisure clothes
der Schuh, -e	shoe
erkennen	to recognize
Sogar meine Freunde erkennen mich manchmal nicht.	Sometimes my friends don't even recognize me.
privat	in private
Privat bin ich ganz anders angezogen.	In my spare time, I dress completely differently.
leicht	light
locker	loose
die Sachen (Pl)	things
Ich mag leichte, lockere Sachen.	I like light and loose things.
bunt	colorful

Seite 87

In der Boutique

die Boutique, -n	boutique, small retail shop
A 3 das Einkaufsgespräch, -e	conversation about shopping
führen	to conduct
Einkaufsgespräche führen	Talking about shopping
stehen	to suit
Meinst du, der Rock steht mir?	Do you think this skirt suits me?
Recht haben	to be right, to be correct
Stimmt, da hast du Recht.	Yes, you are right.
brav	prim

Es ist ein bisschen zu brav.	It is a bit too prim.
ẹcht	really
Also, ich find das echt gut!	Now, I think it is really nice!
ụmsehen	to look around
Wir möchten uns nur umsehen.	We are just looking, thanks.

Im Kaufhaus: Herren-Oberbekleidung

das Kaufhaus, "-er	department store

A 4 das Schaufenster, –	window
ạnprobieren	to try on
Ich möchte den Anzug aus dem Schaufenster anprobieren.	I would like to try on the suit that's in the window.
die Größe, -n	size
Welche Größe?	What size?
drụ̈ben	over there
die Kabịne, -n	changing room
da drüben in der Kabine	over there in the changing room
hụ̈bsch	pretty
Die Bluse sieht hübsch aus.	The blouse looks very pretty.

Tip

Learn adjectives in pairs of opposites.

When you learn a new adjective, familiarize yourself with its opposite. Write sentences accordingly.

sauber – schmutzig
billig – teuer
gut – schlecht

sauber *Die Hose ist sauber.*	*schmutzig* *Sie war schmutzig, ich habe sie gewaschen.*

Seite 88

Früher – heute

A 5 der Stichpunkt, -e	note
Notieren Sie Stichpunkte.	Take notes.
die Latzhose, -n	overall
die Wolle	wool
aussuchen	to choose, to pick out
Ich habe meine Kleider selbst ausgesucht.	I chose my own clothes.
der Vater, "–	father
elegant	elegant, chic
trotzdem	still
doch	yet
der Mode-Fan, -s	fan of fashion
Und ich war doch ein Mode-Fan!	Yet, I was a fan of fashion.
ausziehen	to leave home, to move out
Ich bin von zu Hause ausgezogen.	I left home.
jobben	to work at different jobs
der Musikgeschmack	taste in music
ändern (sich)	to change
Mein Musikgeschmack hat sich geändert.	My taste in music has changed.
statt	instead of
der Programmierer, –	computer programmer
der Minirock, "-e	mini-skirt
die Eltern (Pl)	parents
der Schock	shock
der Karneval	carnival, costume party
die Mutter, "–	mother
dabei	yet
eigen-	own
Dabei habe ich den Rock von meinem eigenen Geld gekauft!	Yet, I bought the skirt with my own money.
d.h. (= das heißt)	that means
ausflippen	to go crasy, to be eccentric
Meine Kleidung war ziemlich ausgeflippt.	My clothes were rather crasy.
deshalb	that is why
der Streit	argument

geben	to give, to be available
es gibt	there is/are
Deshalb hat es Streit gegeben.	That is why there were arguments.
schm**u**tzig	dirty, not clean
norma**l**	normal
Heute bin ich wieder normal.	Now, I'm back to normal again.
die T**o**chter, "–	daughter
verr**ü**ckt	crazy
der H**i**phop	hip hop

Seite 89

Tests

der Test, -s	test

A7	z**u**treffen	to apply to
	Was trifft für Sie zu?	What applies to you?
	der Str**e**ss	stress
	die N**o**te, -n	grade

Hören testen

A8	dr**ei**teilig	3-piece
	kar**ie**rt	checked
	gestr**ei**ft	striped
	einfarbig	unicolored
	h**e**ll	light-colored

Lesen testen

A9	die W**ie**dereröffnung	reopening
	der Str**ei**k, -s	strike
	die Ba**hn**	railway
	das M**o**degeschäft, -e	fashion shop
	geschl**o**ssen sein	to be closed
	Das Geschäft ist heute geschlossen.	The shop is closed today.
	der S**o**nderverkauf, "-e	special sale
	der Comp**u**terraum, "-e	computer room
	zur Verf**ü**gung stehen	to be at disposal

| *Der Computerraum steht zur Verfügung.* | The computer room is at your disposal. |
| der Menüplan, "-e | menu |

Seite 90

Kleidung

A 10 die Badehose, -n	bathing trunks
die Unterhose, -n	underpants
der Bikini, -s	bikini

A 11 nett	nice
eng	tight
die Socke, -n	sock
der Hut, "-e	hat
die Lederjacke, -n	leather jacket
der Schirm, -e	umbrella
das Paar Schuhe	pair of shoes
der Handschuh, -e	glove
der Strumpf, "-e	stocking, knee sock

Koffer packen

der Koffer, –	suitcase
packen	to pack
Koffer packen	to pack a suitcase

| **A 12** einpacken | to pack in, to bring |
| *Ich packe einen Pullover ein.* | I'm bringing a sweater. |

Tip

Practice the endings to the adjectives.

At best, use cards. Here are some suggestions:

| *der Rock – grün* | *der grüne Rock* |
| *Der Rock ist grün.* | *Der grüne Rock steht mir gut.* |

| *Röcke – blau* | *blaue Röcke* |
| *Die Röcke sind blau* | *Die blauen Röcke sind modern.* |

warm	warm
warme Strümpfe	warm stockings
raus	out
Du bist raus.	You are out.

12 Ausklang: Wetter und Landschaften

Seite 94

der Ausklang	end
die Landschaft, -en	region

Die vier Jahreszeiten

die Jahreszeit, -en	season

A1 der Frühling	spring
aktuell	current, up-to-date
Das Skigebiet, -e	skiing area
der Wanderweg, -e	hiking path
das Snowboard , -s	snow board
das Paradies, -e	paradise
europäisch	European
der Fernwanderweg, -e	long distance hiking trail
die Wanderung, -en	hike
der Wald, "-er	forest
der Berg, -e	mountain
die Gletscherwelt, -en	world of glaciers
regnerisch	rainy
kühl	cool
typisch	typical
typisch für die Jahreszeit	typical for this time of year
die Burg, -en	fortress
günstig	affordable, inexpensive
hinaus	out
Ich muss hinaus, ich muss zu dir.	I must go out, I must go to you.
licht (= hell)	light, brilliant
in diesen lichten Tagen	in these brilliant days

A2 die Aktivität, -en	activity

A 3 der Herbst   fall
der Winter   winter

Sonne, Regen, Blitz und Donner

die Sonne	sun
der Regen	rain
der Blitz, -e	lightening
der Donner	thunder

A 4 die Wettervorher-   weather prediction,
  sage, -n   weather forecast
die Karte, -n   map
nachschlagen   to refer to
Schlagen Sie im Wörterbuch   Refer to the dictionary.
  nach.
sonnig   sunny
heiter   bright
wolkig   cloudy
stark   very
bewölkt   partly cloudy
stark bewölkt   very cloudy
der Regenschauer, –   shower
das Gewitter, –   thunderstorm
der Nebel   fog
der Schneefall, "-e   snowfall

Tip

Combine words with pictures.

Draw symbols of the weather. Write the German word for
these symbols and list the "weather words" on a scale from
good to bad.

regnerisch ⟶ sonnig
der Regen

Der Jahreszeiten-Maler

A 5 blühen	to bloom
Ich lass meine Blumen blühen.	I let my flowers bloom.
Ostern	Easter
lieb sein	to be kind
spinnen	to be unpredictable
Bei uns spinnt der April.	In April, we have unpredictable weather here.
egal	whatever
egal was dann passiert	whatever happens then
die Wolke, -n	cloud
so viel	so much
Wir können so viel machen.	We can do so much.
wild	crazy, wild
Sie finden mein Bild zu wild?	Do you think my painting is too crazy?
tot	dead, deceased
der Tau	dew
der Schnee	snow
das Eis	ice
schneien	to snow
Wenn es noch schneit in unsern Breiten, . . .	When it still snows in our region, . . .
die Apfelsine, -n	orange

A 6 der Wortigel, –	hedge hog of words

Spiel: Was Sie schon immer wissen wollten . . .

das Spiel, -e	game

A 7 würfeln	to play dice, to throw dice
Würfeln Sie noch einmal.	Throw the dice again.
der Zuhörer, –	listener
die Zuhörerin, -nen	listener
bewerten	to keep points, to keep score
Bewerten Sie in der Gruppe.	Be the score keeper for the group.
die Punktzahl	score

der Start	start
das Ziel	end
der Punkt, -e	point
die Fremdsprache, -n	foreign language
der Joker, –	joker
der Würfel, –	dice
die Lieblingsmusik	favorite music
der Arbeitsplatz, "-e	workplace
der Urlaub, -e	vacation, holiday
das nächste Mal, -e	the next time
die Regel, -n	rule
der Sieger, –	winner
die Siegerin, -nen	winner
der Spieler, –	player
die Spielerin, -nen	player
das Feld, -er	square
das Ende	end
Das Spiel ist zu Ende.	The game is over.
die Gratulation, -en	congratulation
Gratulation!	Congratulations!

Tip

Learn words in rhyme pairs.

Collect words that rhyme and write them in pairs.

rund und bunt
essen und vergessen
mir und dir

Spannung im DaF-Unterricht

Leichte Lektüren

Donauwalzer
Stufe 1, illustriert, 48 Seiten
ISBN 3-468-49700-8

Berliner Pokalfieber
Stufe 1, illustriert, 40 Seiten
ISBN 3-468-49705-9

Der Märchenkönig
Stufe 1, illustriert, 40 Seiten
ISBN 3-468-49706-7

Heidelberger Herbst
Stufe 2, illustriert, 48 Seiten
ISBN 3-468-49708-3

Tatort Frankfurt
Stufe 2, illustriert, 48 Seiten
ISBN 3-468-49707-5

Anruf genügt ... und Privatdetektiv
Helmut Müller aus Berlin ist zur
Stelle.
Er spielt die Hauptrolle in der
Krimi-Reihe von Felix und Theo.
Spannende Kriminallektüren in
drei Schwierigkeitsstufen für
Deutsch-Lernende aller Alters-
stufen.
Jeder Band enthält im Anhang
einen Übungsteil, der Hilfestellung
bei der Inhaltserschließung gibt.

Infos & mehr
www.langenscheidt.de

Langenscheidt
...weil Sprachen verbinden